Contents

Introduction 2

What Is Forex or Currency Exchange? 5

Demand And Supply 8

What Is The Graph And What Exactly Do You See? 14

Let's Move Casual For a Second: 2 Strategies 21

    Breakout 21

    Trend Is Your Best Friend 24

Analyzing the News or How Not to Trade the News 27

Think in flowers - trading psychology 30

Price Action Worth Knowing 32

Conclusion 34

Introduction

Let's start with "who am I and why you should trust me". I've been trading on a market for about 3 to 4 years (Once you hear that somebody has 10 years or more at the market and wants your money about his product – stay away! He's probably broken or and has 1 week on the market. People with 10 years of experience rarely want your money), I've been reading lots of books and I've been developing my own strategies. However, I understood that nothing is permanent. Why? Simply because of the market - it changes, because of the people. People make the market, they construct the price - simply said they control the demand and supply of the current goods (in our case assets) on the market. Currency market makes no difference. The demand and supply law is something that we will discuss later, but for now what you must know is that this is the most important (the only) thing that forms the price.

Before starting university, I was already trading by almost a year and a half and I felt happy with my results. I entered the binary options industry and worked there for a while. When I started studying economics at the university, I understood that things are a little bit different than I thought. Back then I was only using technical analysis because I didn't understand what the fundamental analysis is. Yes, I knew it's about the GDP and CPI and the interest rates that the Banks set, but I didn't understand it perfectly.

I was trading like an algorithm and when found out about algorithms I was very curious why there were still people that were trading by themselves. And the reason is this: market changes and so your algorithm must change. After my first year at the university, I started as a financial analyst and I used to give predictions to the clients of the company. Then I understood that many people gave predictions about the prices, but almost none of them were accurate in the long run. They were trying to predict the market using algorithms. Using **one algorithm**, in the long run, **does not predict human behavior**. In the short run - yes, that's why I was successful in my first year (successful for me was 40% on a yearly basis). Now I'm trading mostly with stocks and Forex and my target is much lower. Why? We will speak about this one later, now I would like to share some of my results from a tiny account I used to manage:

From: 2018-07-16	To: 2018-08-15								
Asset	Quantity	Direction	Rate	Close Rate	Date	Close Date	Swap	Commission	Result
EUR/USD	70000	SellToClose	1.13099	1.13184	2018-08-15 14:25:56	2018-08-15 14:26:00	€	€ 0	€ 52.33
EUR/USD	30000	BuyToClose	1.14242	1.14236	2018-08-13 13:31:05	2018-08-13 13:31:00	€	€ 0	€ 1.67
EUR/USD	10000	SellToClose	1.13749	1.13770	2018-08-13 08:25:40	2018-08-13 08:26:00	€	€ 0	€ 1.85
EUR/USD	10000	BuyToClose	1.14722	1.14710	2018-08-10 09:18:50	2018-08-10 09:19:00	€	€ 0	€ 1.03
GBP/USD	30000	SellToClose	1.27541	1.27544	2018-08-10 08:59:46	2018-08-10 09:00:00	€	€ 0	€ 0.78
EUR/USD	10000	SellToClose	1.14615	1.14549	2018-08-10 07:43:33	2018-08-10 07:44:00	€	€ 0	€ 2.95
GBP/USD	5000	SellToClose	1.28886	1.28903	2018-08-09 12:22:04	2018-08-09 12:22:00	€	€ 0	€ 0.73
GBP/USD	5000	BuyToClose	1.28908	1.28853	2018-08-09 09:59:12	2018-08-09 09:59:00	€	€ 0	€ 2.37
EUR/USD	1000	SellToClose	1.15912	1.15948	2018-08-08 09:47:51	2018-08-08 09:48:00	€	€ 0	€ 0.31
AUD/USD	3000	BuyToClose	0.74345	0.74302	2018-08-07 13:38:30	2018-08-07 13:38:00	€	€ 0	€ 1.13
USD/CAD	30000	SellToClose	1.29695	1.29700	2018-08-07 09:09:38	2018-08-07 09:10:00	€	€ 0	€ 0.93
EUR/USD	10000	SellToClose	1.15350	1.15362	2018-08-06 11:52:45	2018-08-06 11:53:00	€	€ 0	€ 1.04
Apple	50	SellToClose	206.444	207.220	2018-08-03 14:40:36	2018-08-03 14:41:00	€	€ 8.94	€ 33.46
Facebook	50	SellToClose	178.270	178.844	2018-08-06 13:58:28	2018-08-06 13:58:00	€	€ 7.73	€ 24.74
EUR/USD	1000	SellToClose	1.15865	1.15704	2018-08-03 13:29:37	2018-08-03 13:30:00	€	€ 0	€ 1.38
Facebook	100	SellToClose	172.020	174.620	2018-08-02 16:30:37	2018-08-02 16:31:00	€	€ 14.98	€ 223.08
Gold	60	SellToClose	1225.49	1222.80	2018-08-02 16:30:37	2018-08-02 16:31:00	€	€ 0	-€ 138.17
GBP/USD	5000	SellToClose	1.30832	1.30394	2018-08-02 16:30:37	2018-08-02 16:31:00	€	€ 0	-€ 18.79
Dow Jones Future	1	SellToClose	25304.500	25260.000	2018-08-02 16:30:37	2018-08-02 16:31:00	€	€ 0	-€ 40.05
S&P Future	1	SellToClose	2809.250	2821.000	2018-08-02 16:30:37	2018-08-02 16:31:00	€	€ 0	€ 10.58
NASDAQ 100 Future	2	SellToClose	7275.450	7354.500	2018-08-02 16:30:37	2018-08-02 16:31:00	€	€ 0	€ 134.39
Johnson & Johnson	11	SellToClose	132.4259	132.5200	2018-08-02 16:30:37	2018-08-02 16:31:00	€	€ 5	€ 0.85
Microsoft	11	SellToClose	106.143	107.310	2018-08-02 16:30:36	2018-08-02 16:31:00	€	€ 5	€ 10.97
BMW	1	SellToClose	81.7000	80.9100	2018-08-02 16:30:36	2018-08-02 16:31:00	€	€ 5	-€ 0.79
EUR/USD	1000	BuyToClose	1.16900	1.16890	2018-08-01 13:08:07	2018-08-01 13:08:00	€	€ 0	€ 0.09
Total:	221287.00							€ 47	€ 308.86

The initial deposit on this account was €10 000. The priority of this account were stocks, but I decided to give him forex signals so he can cover some of his commission. You may ask: "OK, why don't you trade only forex?" and the answer is: Why

4

should I trade only on one market when I see opportunities on others. I am also going to publish another book that will be entirely about stocks, but for this one, we will be discussing only currencies.

There are several main questions you should ask yourself before entering this big world that has a turnover of almost $5 trillion a day:

- What is Forex?
- Why does it exist?
- Why not everybody makes money out of it?

What Is Forex or Currency Exchange?

" Forex is a decentralized market for money." - simple definition. Why would people buy or sell money? Let's say that you want to go on vacation. You're from Europe and your country uses entirely euro and you want to go to the United States. Obviously, you need to exchange Euro for US Dollar and you need the marketplace for that. Here is where our market enters the game. You are buying dollars (selling EUR/USD) for somebody who wants euros and is selling his dollars to you (buying EUR/USD). You both are happy. That's all? No. For this market to have 5 trillion dollars turnover there should be something else than two guys who want to go on a vacation. Yes, and this is the following: Banks, Companies, Hedge Funds, and Speculators.

We should keep in mind what banks would do, news about the companies and we should trade like a Hedge fund. Through monetary policy, banks directly set the price of money. Through their needs and contracts, companies influence indirectly the price of money. Hedge funds keep in mind these things, so if we keep them in mind, we may be able to trade like a hedge fund. Speculators? Oh, that's us. We are there for the money. We do not influence the market -

sorry (or at least we do not have that much impact as the other major participants). The major market participants exchange currencies because they must in order to reach their goals. For example, if Apple wants to buy a certain type of technology from IBM Europe, it must exchange USD for EUR (buying EUR/USD).

And the most important question is why not everybody makes money when they learn the basics? Because of two reasons - greed and fear. You are making some money - you are becoming greedy and do not follow the plan, you are losing some money - you want to take out your money and end the game.

Of course, these feelings are normal. When you know how much money could be made, it's logical to become greedy and when you see how fast you can lose money, it's logical to become scared. That's why we have money management (something that almost no one is using on the market and the main reason 90% of people lose their money).

Later, we will speak about money management in details. For now, you must know that this is the key to successful trading. The next most import thing you must understand is the law of demand and supply.

Demand and Supply

The law of demand and supply is an assumption that simplifies the connection between the demand for a resource and the supply for that resource. The law describes the effect that the availability of an exact product and the desire (or demand) of that product have on its price. Generally speaking, low demand and high supply result in a decrease in the price. In contrast, the greater the demand and the lower the supply, the price tends to increase.

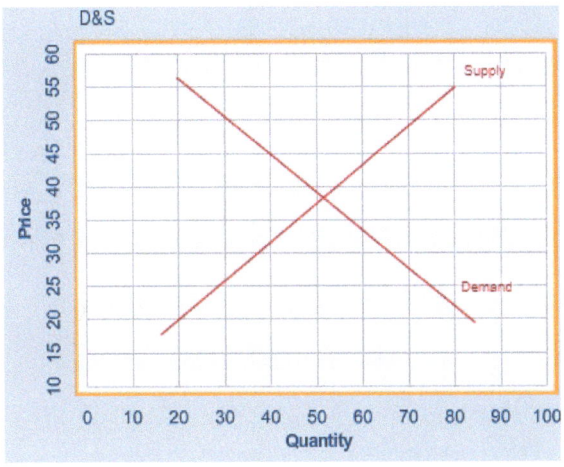

So basically, we care about is the price. As already discussed, we are speculators. This means that were there to buy low and sell high. For now, we know that the month and supply influence the price, and this is the only thing that influences the price. Everything else that happens in the world influences the demand and the supply, but it does not directly influence the price. This is the basic market structure for almost every market, but let's close a little bit the circle and make it specific. We're going to analyze the demand and the supply in the market of money.

9

There the supply curve is a little bit different, it is vertical and is mostly influenced by the Central Bank.

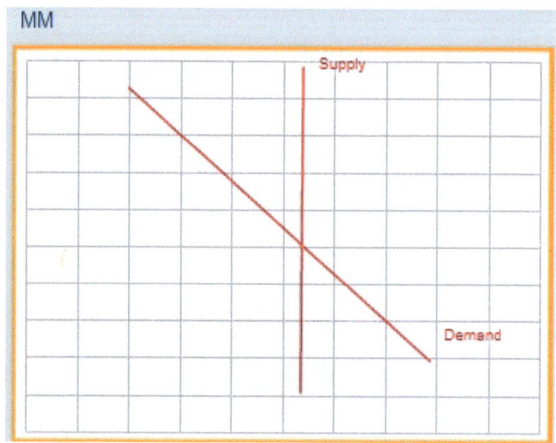

Now, from the supply side, we know that we should care about the Central Banks - what they say, what they plan to do (do they plan to increase the rates or no). Why exactly do we care about the interest rates? This is the price of money. If I ask you how much a euro does costs, you're probably going to compare it to other currency (for example one euro costs X dollars). The price of money is the interest rate that you pay to the bank for the money you loaned. If we analyze it from the eyes of a borrower, that would be the price of money. Well, as traders we are borrowers. Think about it - you borrow a certain amount of euros for dollars in order to sell them at a better rate and make a profit out of it. That is the reason why when the Fed (Federal Reserve - the Central Bank of USA) says that they are going to increase the rates the USD pairs go up (in the case of EUR/USD - it goes down).

So, the price of money, in the long run, is decided by the central banks (of course if nothing else changes). If there is World War III, the things change (but I guess that then Forex trading would be your last problem). And here I reviewed one of my strategies - read what banks publish (and by banks, I mean central banks) and act according to it. You can look at the economic calendar (which could be found at many websites) and search for the central banks meeting. If you don't want to read the report, there is a smarter way to understand what they said. Just look at the chat - if there is one green big candle, they said something in favor of the bull (long or it's time to buy), if there is one big red candle, they said something in favor of the bear (short or it's time to sell). Keep in mind that for this strategy to be effective you must keep the trade for a longer period than usual. This is a less stressful way to trade. You open one trade and do not look at it until it's time to close it (usually before the next meeting of the central bank).

So, we spoke about the supply side, let's speak a little bit about the demand. We're going to analyze the example that we gave in the first chapter - the example with IBM Europe and Apple. And for purpose of this analysis, we're going to assume that the contract is directly made with IBM Europe which only works with Euro.

So, Apple now needs to purchase euro to make the transaction and to finish the contract. Therefore, the demand for a euro should increase, and the price of a euro should increase as well (everything else held constant). So here comes another "I heard from the news" strategy. If you hear from somewhere that giant companies are making a contract and both companies are situated in different countries which has a different major currency, then you should analyze it as we analyze it from the example above. This kind of contracts cannot happen without the market of money: therefore, they have an impact on the demand. This strategy has a lot of "haters", but I can tell that from the last 5 trades I made with the strategy, 5 of them were successful.

Using this strategy, you're entering at the exact moment that should be entered because they announce the contract and after that, they transfer the money and it's a long process. The big money moves slow. There are even times that the whole payment is made on several payments. With this kind of thinking is hard to be late. You should be careful about are the other things that happened in the market. As every strategy, we say, "everything else held constant" and here it is very hard for everything else to hold constant.

So, after I showed you some simple economics graphs, let's understand what we actually see on our platforms.

What Is the Graph and What Exactly Do You See?

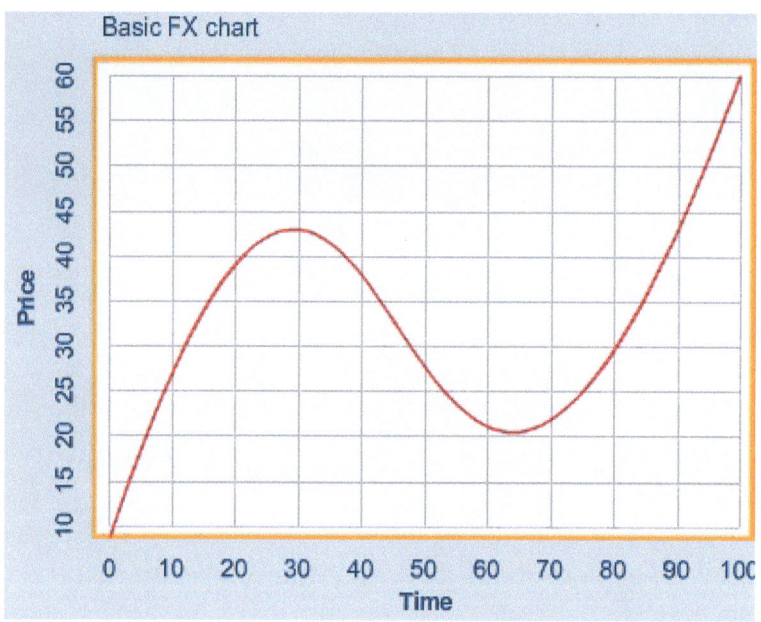

Every graph has the purpose of showing a relationship. The graph of our platforms shows the relationship between time and price.

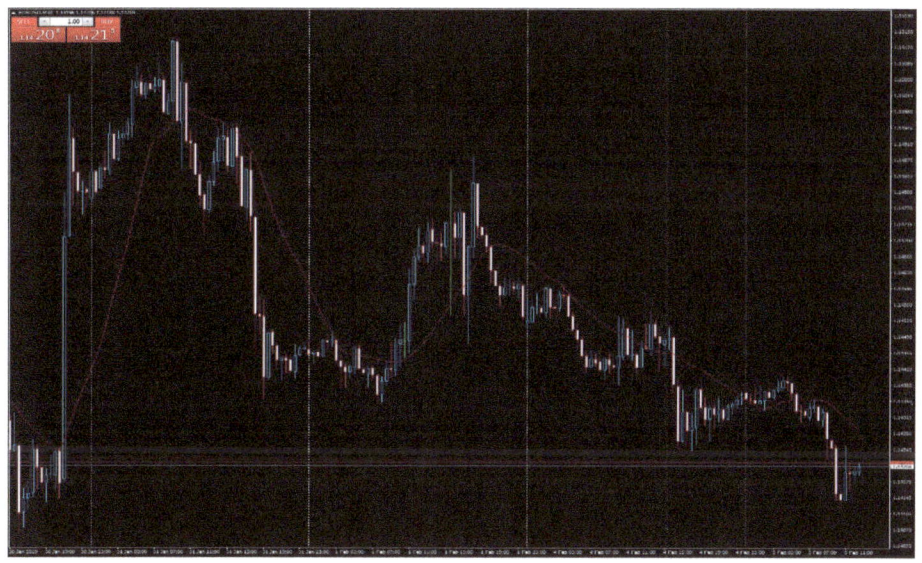

How does time help us analyzing the price? The velocity of price changing is very important and very useful if we try trading using price action. The reason behind this is that we understand (or at least we assume) who may be placing orders and why. If the big money is on the table, there's something that forms, and it's called impulse. Everything else is a correction.

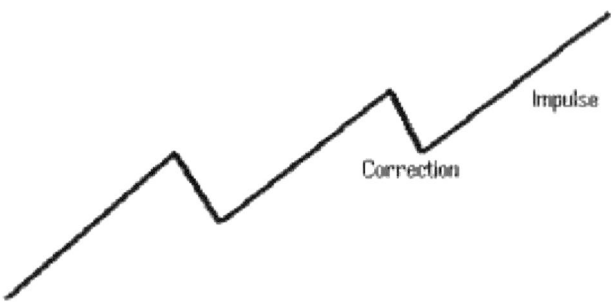

This is the basics behind Elliott's Waves Theory. The truth about this theory is that almost nobody understands it the way that it must be understood. You're going to see many people offering you Elliott wave signals but trust me if you call three different wave traders showing you waves in the graph, you're going to see three different "images". What you should know for now is that after an impulse, there is a correction and forming an impulse takes more time than forming a correction.

Maybe this is the time to explain what an indicator is. An indicator is a mathematical function, which variable is the price and it's used by traders to predict the price changes. The logic behind it and behind the whole technical analysis is that the past tends to repeat itself. The logic behind my analysis is that people try to change the future, knowing the past. Who tries to change it? The people that are known as the Big Money (for example central banks trying to predict a crisis and to prevent it).

My personal favorite indicators are SMA (simple moving average), RSI (relative strength index) and ATR (average true range). The first two indicators are important because many people look at them and they show very useful information. The ATR for me is an indicator that could help you predict the price changes (usually it is not used for that). How we said earlier there's an impulse and a correction, so the price cannot move only in one direction for a whole day/week/month (sometimes even an hour). For example, if the average true range shows that the average range is 100 pips and it's already moving for like 98 pips up, I will place a sell order and hopefully, it will hit my Take Profit.

A simple moving average is a simplistic type of moving average in financial analysis. It is determined by summing up the last "N" period's closing prices and then dividing the whole by N. If you set a 20 period SMA on a 30-minute chart, you would add up the closing prices for the last 10 hours (20 multiplied by 30 minutes or 0.5 hours), and then divide that number by 20. Now you have found the average price over the last 10 hours illustrated on the chart. Combining those average prices and you will get a function - moving average.

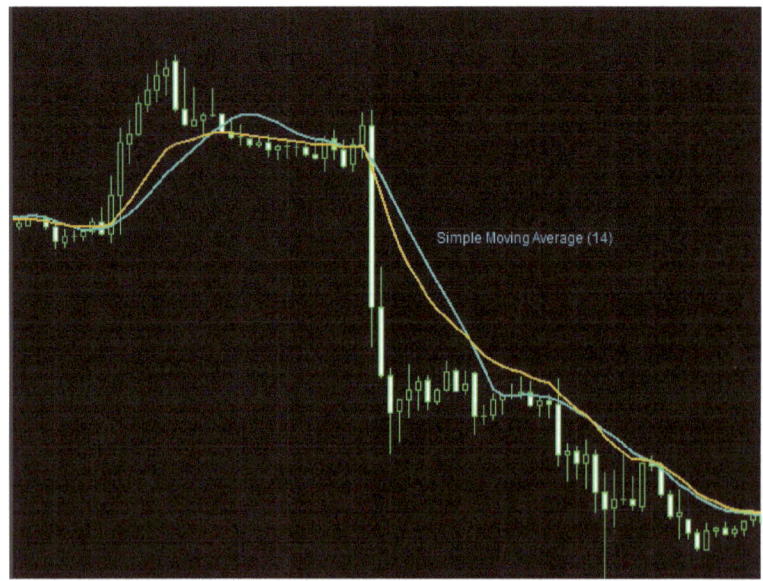

Relative Strength Index is a common indicator that assists traders to evaluate the strength of the market. It is estimated from zero to hundred. Readings of 30 and below means that the market is at oversold conditions and there is an increase in the possibility of price strengthening (going up). Traders understand that an oversold currency pair is a piece of evidence that the declining trend is expected to reverse, which opens an opportunity to buy. Readings of 70 and higher show overbought conditions and increase the possibility of the price going down. Some traders understand that an overbought currency pair is a piece of evidence that the growing trend is expected to reverse, which means it opens an opportunity to sell.

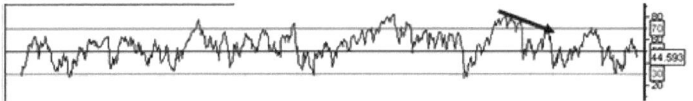

The Average True Range is an indicator to mathematically estimate the volatility of price fluctuations. At first, it was used for the commodities market wherever volatility is a lot of prevailing. However, it's currently wide utilized by forex traders furthermore. Traders seldom use the indicator to tell apart expected price movement directions, nevertheless, use it to realize a perception of what recent historical volatility is to arrange an execution plan for trading. Setting stops and entry points at key levels to predict where they may be stopped out or whipsawed are edges of this indicator.

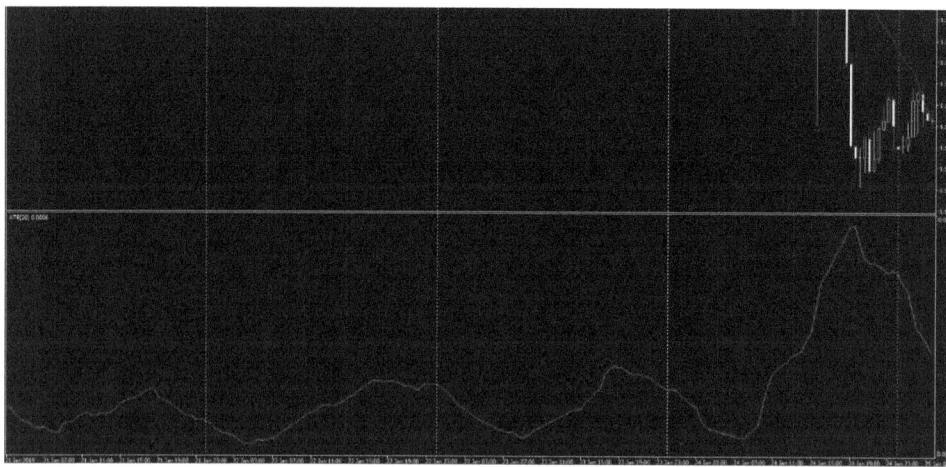

Let's Move Casual for a Second: 2 Strategies

Now, let's take a break from all this theory and economics and jump a little bit into trading. In this chapter, I will present you 2 strategies that are very simple to follow and still very effective. **Remember!** If you start practicing one of them, be disciplined. This is what makes a trader profitable in the long-run.

Breakout

Markets seldom oscillate within support and resistance bands. This is identified as consolidation. A break is when the market moves exceeding the limits of its consolidation, towards new heights or minimums. When a brand-new trend happens, a break must first occur. Accordingly, outbreaks are potential signals that a new trend has begun. But the dilemma is that not any breakouts produce new trends. Even these easy approaches should be practiced with risk management (for which we will speak later). It seeks to reduce its losses through the breakdown of the trend. A new peak indicates the possibility that an uptrend is starting, and a new minimum show that a downward trend is starting.

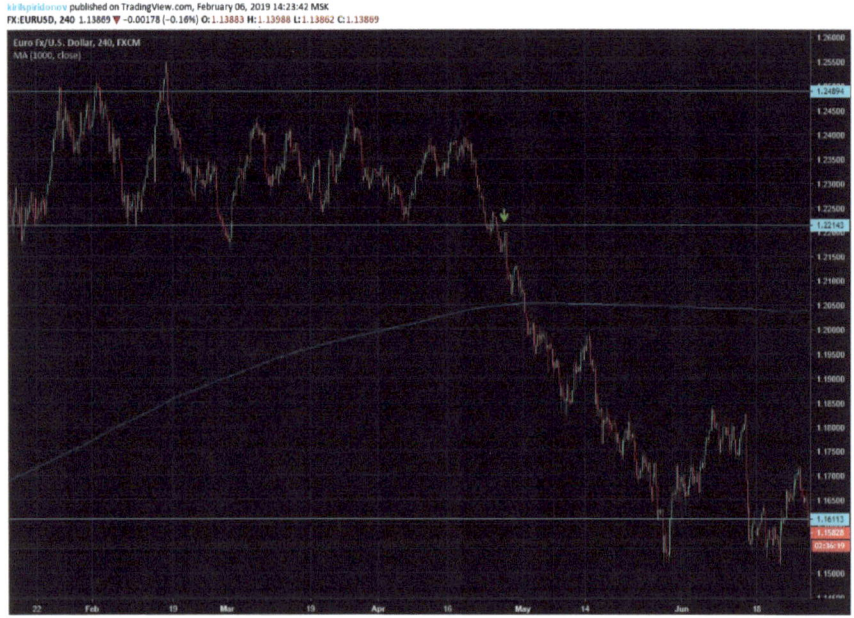

The continuance of the period gives us the possibility to define the highest height or the lowest low. A break past the above maximum or the below minimum over a longer duration proposes a longer trend. A breakout for a short period of time hints a mid-term or a short-term trend. Therefore, you can settle a breakout plan to react quickly or slowly to the creation of a trend. Reacting faster lets you chase a trend earlier in the curve but may result in following the wrong trends and results in losses.

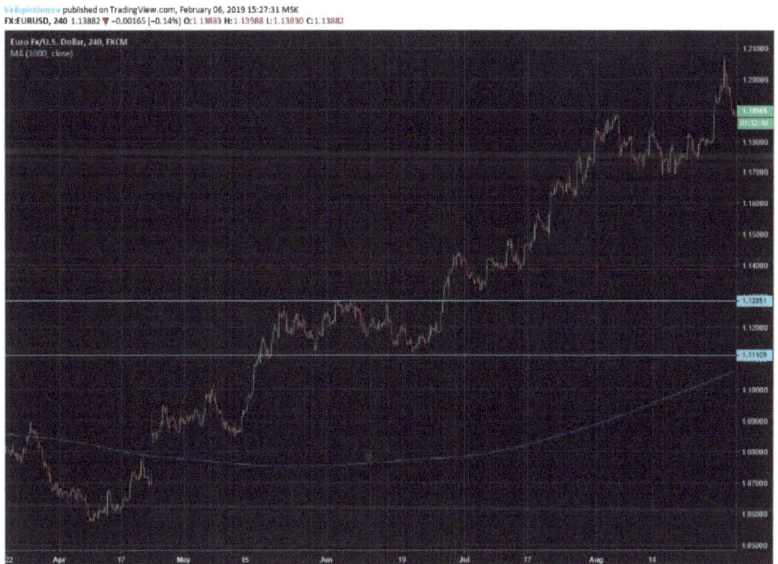

Trend Is Your Best Friend

Trends tell us where the market is going — in the trend. Also, because we know that upward trends increase, we can take advantage of the information to put variables, stop losses and potential targets. The following statement is a strategic low-risk trend for forex trading but requires proof that a trend is in place. For a downward trend, we'd like to see a pullback below the previous high, and another fall right to a new low below the previous one. We look to enter on the next pullback once that pattern has reappeared. We keep doing that as long as the price is lower and lower.

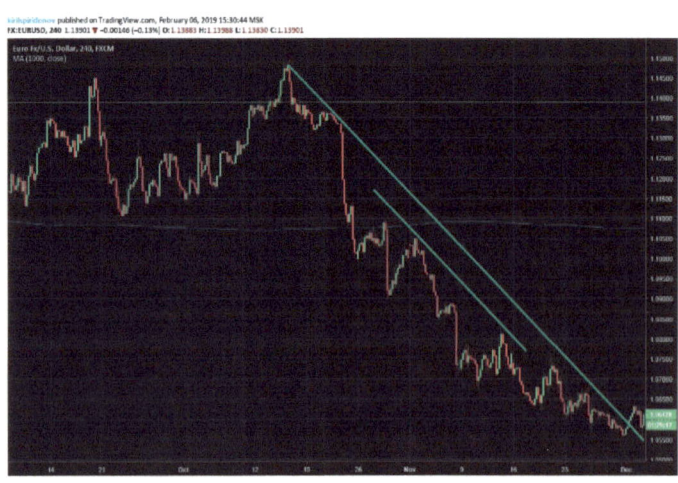

In an upward trend, we must see an upward pullback, a move that stays above the previous downward swing, then an upward pullback. That gives enough evidence to start searching for signals after this pattern has evolved. After seeing the price make the necessary moves, we look to buy at the next pullback. While the price is higher and lower, we continue going long (buying)

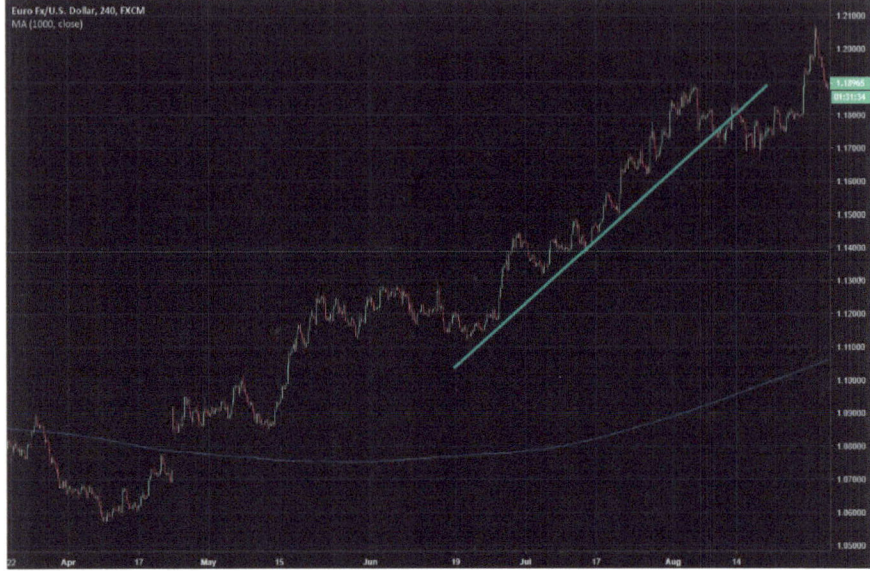

We're never going to be perfect all the time, but we can enhance our chances with some new tools. A trendline is sometimes useful, but only when the price of the trend bounced off. Set a stop loss slightly lower than the pre-entry swing. A take profit slightly exceeds the past swing high. This is the most conservative target and provides us with the greatest chance of being profitable. A more aggressive strategy is trying to extract more profit by raising the price of the primary target.

Trendlines and channels are not always useful, because the lows are not always aligned with a global trend. We can use other instruments to assist us in our trade decisions if this happens. Then we really want the trend, plus of course the direct trade signal, and some other proof about the trade signal itself. Typical levels (a.k.a. retracement levels) are included in these tools (indicators like the RSI or tools like Fibonacci Retracement). Another great tool for defining a trend is SMA. When the price is above the SMA it should be analyzed as a bull trend, if it is below the SMA it should be analyzed as a bearish trend.

Analyzing the News or How Not to Trade the News

A trader, and especially trading forex, is facing a difficult challenge to find perspective. It is difficult enough to achieve that on regular hour markets, but Forex is exceptionally painstaking when prices move 24 hours a day, 7 days a week. It is difficult to separate yourself from the action and avoid unnecessary responses to the market when flooded with constantly changing market data. Your feelings are not important to the market. Speculators have heard it in other ways— you can only influence it when you buy and sell. It is easier to know how to not trade than how to trade in direct response to that statement.

News are speculative, don't just read them, you must understand what the meaning behind them is. Usually, news releases from public agencies are truly a vehicle for a certain point of view or policy. In currency markets, such "real" news is more used than any other tool for affecting the audience's capital investment psychology. Inherently, this kind of media manipulation is not always pessimistic. Politicians and speculators are always trying to use it. A completely new forex trader should be aware of the importance of reading the news in order to evaluate the message.

You must understand what stays behind the message, how the messenger delivery information and why this important person is saying this to the public, differently said - what he wants to say to the major players on the financial market. Sometimes something negative can turn to be very positive and something very positive can turn out to be very negative. Read the papers with the viewpoint that, in forex, how the event is reported can be as crucial as the event itself.

Sometimes, when trading the news, you may see a certain type of movements that are very aggressive and unpredictable. They are very big, sharp and can kill your portfolio (a.k.a. surges). A price surge is a signature of panic or surprise. In these events, professional traders take cover and see what happens.

The retail trader also should let the market digest such shocks. Trading during an announcement or right before, or amid some turmoil, minimizes the odds of predicting the probable direction. Technical indicators during surge periods will be distorted. You should wait for a confirmation of the new direction and remember that price action will tend to revert to pre-surge ranges providing nothing fundamental has occurred.

Think in flowers - trading psychology

We arrive at your relationship with money after minimizing your exposure. Like that or not, in our society money is highly appreciated. This is important. And we give it a lot of feeling. So how would you feel when you see thousands of dollars disappearing before you? The issue is that "cost" is part of this game. To earn a little more, you have to lose a little. There is no 100% winning strategy. If you can't change your mindset about money, don't think about it. Concentrate on percentages change. Think about profit as money. Think of the average risk-reward ratio. Think about everything as a percentage, not directly as money.

The other way to think of money is like trading flowers. At the moment you put money in your account, you are buying with them flowers. You are

trading from this moment with flowers. Once, you input that mindset into your brain, your trading will become a lot easier.

The more money you spend, the more emotional fuel you fill the fire. You'll sooner or later be burned... Unfairly. And it can be irreparable post-traumatic stress. In the hope of a quick win, most beginning traders risk far too much. Experienced and skilled traders are better informed. A couple of big losers can eat you alive rapidly in day trading, where transactions can come in from everywhere. Good day traders who survive risk only a small amount of trading capital at all in any trade. If you are "illiquid, "consider using a trading system that gives a tight loss of stoppage. Put differently, trade a shorter period in which losses can be minimized, such as a 5-minute chart.

Overconfidence is another factor that influences your risk estimation and pushes you to make mistakes. If tails have come up 10 times in a row that does not mean that you must put half the trading capital on heads. Sometimes emotions make you see something as a sure trade but follow the risk management, even when it's sure. Remember, your highest priority is to build up a system that works in the long-run.

Price Action Worth Knowing – Double Tops and Bottoms

In nearly every market and time frame, two tops and double bottoms often appear and are fantastic indicators of a potential reversal of trends. I like these price models because they offer a logical entry and exit and frequently quickly reach the target price. As the name implies, this pattern includes two peaks with approximately the same height for the dual top formation and two bottoms with approximately equal depth for dual bottom structure.

Double "ups" are sometimes referred to as "M 's" and double downs "W's" because the pattern is like each letter. They are contra-trend patterns and, when the previous trend is stronger, the greater the reverse. Statistics show that the duration of the double tops is also shorter, and the movement is more pronounced. On the other hand, double bottoms tend to last longer.

The next and most crucial part of the pattern is that the neckline breaks and closes underneath the neckline. It is important to close the neckline, as the market can only be consolidated up to that point.

Then you have two choices once the neckline is clearly broken. You can enter the market right away or wait to see if the newly formed resistor is reverted to the neckline. If the market returns to the neckline, it's usually good to get to your position even further (open another one).

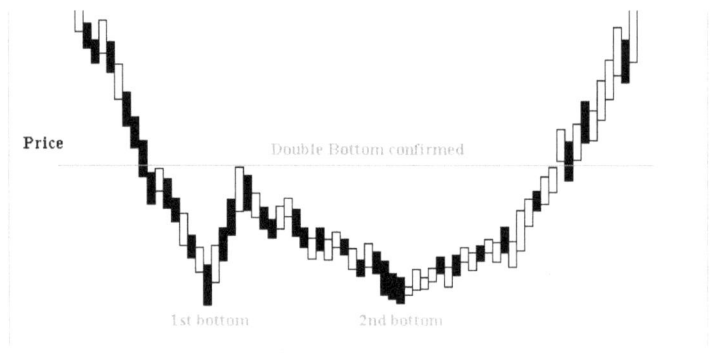

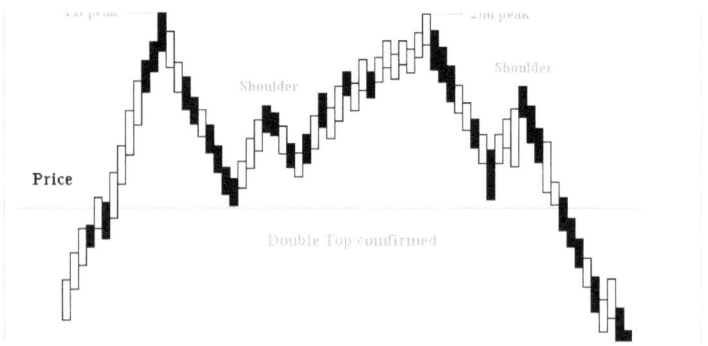

Conclusion

To master trading, it costs a lot of practice, therefore it costs money, but it's like every other education. Traders pay for their education through losses, so don't be afraid to lose at first. What is more important is to understand where your mistakes are. Of course, sometimes keep in mind that the market may be against you and it's ok it's not your fault. Do the things in this book that I've told you for at least half a year and be disciplined during that period. Also, do not forget that market changes, so we must keep an eye on everything that happens.

It was a pleasure for me to write this book. Wish you best luck on the market!

www.ingramcontent.com/pod-product-compliance
Lightning Source LLC
Chambersburg PA
CBHW040341220526
45473CB00009B/2754